Published by
Gallery Books
An imprint of W H Smith Publishers Inc.
112 Madison Avenue
New York, New York 10016 USA

Produced by
Twin Books
15 Sherwood Place
Greenwich, CT 06830 USA

ISBN 0-8317-2302-5

Printed in Hong Kong

Fun with Words

In the City

Twin Books

GALLERY BOOKS
An imprint of W.H. Smith Publishers Inc.
112 Madison Avenue
New York, New York 10016

THINGS WITH WHEELS

So many toys have wheels, and all of them are fun.

Baby Gyro has fastened his  together

to make a new kind of toy. What will he do next ?

Baby Goofy has fallen right off his .

Luckily, he isn't hurt. Baby Donald can go very

fast on his . He and Baby Daisy are

going to have a race. She has training wheels on

her  to help her balance. They are all

making a lot of noise, but somehow Baby Minnie is

still asleep in her . Maybe she

is just pretending.

Bicycle

Scooter

Skateboard

Roller Skates

Doll Carriage

HOW WE GO

The Disney Babies are playing with their cars and

trucks. "Beep, beep !" says Baby Goofy, pushing

his  across the rug. Baby Mickey has

stopped his van at the stop sign. Now he will play

with the big orange  . What fun !

Baby Gyro is planning to build a track for the little

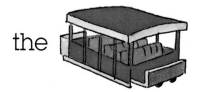 . Baby Daisy and Baby Minnie join the

game by loading blocks into the back of a  .

Then they will put the toy figures on the chair into

the underneath it. Soon there will

be a traffic jam !

Truck

Trolley

Bus

Taxicab

Train

OUR PLAYGROUND

The Disney Babies love to go to the playground.

Baby Minnie thinks the  is the most fun,

but she needs a push to get started. Baby Goofy

is riding a horse on the . He

calls to Baby Donald to join him, but Baby Donald

is on the  with Baby Mickey. Baby Mickey

has tied a rock to his end to make it heavier, so

Baby Donald has to hold on tightly. In the

Baby Daisy is building castles. Baby Gyro is waiting

at the top of the  until she's finished, but

Baby Pete is right behind him.

Merry-go-round

Swing

Seesaw

Slide

Sandbox

EATING OUT

Baby Minnie is looking at the  so she can

choose her favorite food. Baby Daisy is sitting

in her ![chair] beside her, tying her napkin

around her neck as a bib. Baby Gyro has called

the ![baby waiter] , who turns out to be Baby Donald.

He is carefully bringing some cupcakes on a round

![plate] . Baby Gyro thinks they look very good.

Baby Mickey is stirring something on the stove

because he is the ![chef Mickey] . The Disney Babies

like to pretend they are at a restaurant together. It

makes everything taste even better.

Menu

Highchair

Tray

Waiter

Cook

AT THE GYM

The Disney Babies are getting a lot of exercise at the

gym. Baby Gyro is playing on the  ,

which is too big for him to jump over. Baby Mickey

is bouncing on the  . He feels as if

he were flying. Baby Daisy is having trouble

getting onto the . Someone will

have to give her a hand. Baby Pete wants to climb

the , but it's harder than it looks. Baby

Donald is wondering if he can pick up the heavy

barbell. Baby Minnie is enjoying a workout on

the . It's fun at the gym.

Trampoline

Balance Beam

Rope

Vaulting Horse

Exercise Mat

OUR PARK

What a lovely day to play in the park. Baby

Mickey is feeding the ducks in the  .

Another bird is waiting his turn for food –

the hopeful little  . Baby Pete and

Baby Donald are splashing each other with water

to keep cool. Baby Daisy would rather fly her

 . She's very happy that there is a

nice breeze to keep it from falling into the

. Baby Minnie thinks the park is a

great place to look at her book on a tree-shaded

 . What do you like to do in the park ?

Kite

Bench

Fountain

Pond

Pigeon

VISITING THE DOCTOR

It's time for a check-up, and Baby Mickey is

the doctor. He is listening to Baby Donald's heart

through his  . Baby Clarabelle is wearing

a white cap because she is the nurse. She has taken

Baby Horace's temperature with the

that she keeps in the first-aid kit. She is showing him

the , but she will be very careful

with it. Baby Goofy has bandaged himself so tightly

that he can hardly move. Sitting on the  ,

Baby Minnie can't believe she weighs that much.

She doesn't know that Baby Pete is sitting on it, too.

Thermometer

Tongue
Depressor

Stethoscope

Scale

VISITING THE HOSPITAL

Poor Baby Donald has hurt his foot. Baby

Mickey is looking at an  of it to

see what is wrong. When Baby Donald's foot

is better, he will be able to get out of the

 . Until then, Baby Daisy will

be his nurse. She is taking good care of

him and has given him a  . Now she

is wrapping up his foot in a great big

 . Baby Minnie is holding the tape.

When the bandage is finished, they will cut

off the end with the .

X-ray

Scissors

Pill

Wheelchair

Bandage

WORKERS WE SEE

Many jobs involve using different tools.

Baby Goofy wants to be a plumber, so he is

carrying a pipe and a  . Baby Daisy

works in the garden, planting a pretty flower.

First she puts it in a  . Then she waters it.

Baby Donald, the fireman, has a heavy helmet, a

waterproof coat and a . Baby Minnie

has a barber shop, where she cuts hair and

styles it with her . Baby Gyro is a

policeman. He stops traffic with his

so that people can cross the street safely.

Comb

Whistle

Fire Hose

Wrench

Flower Pot

WORKERS IN TOWN

Baby Minnie is working as a secretary who

types business letters on a 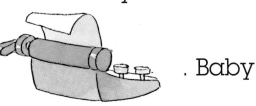 . Baby

Donald, the window washer, cleans and polishes

the office windows with a . Baby Daisy

works at the department store, helping Baby

Clarabelle choose a new of perfume.

Baby Goofy, the businessman, is wearing a suit.

He keeps all sorts of important papers in his

 . He has stopped at the bank with

a check, so that Baby Mickey, who is his banker,

can give him  in return.

ON OUR STREET

The Disney Babies are taking a walk along their

street. Baby Goofy is waiting by the  sign.

He wonders if there is a bus coming along soon.

When the street is empty, they will cross safely at

the  . Maybe they will hold hands and

help one another as they step off and onto the

 . On the sidewalk, they will have to keep

their eyes open and be careful not to bump into

the . In this part of town, they

must also watch out for the tall

which stand like giant trees.

Telephone Poles

STOP

Fire Hydrant

Crosswalk

BUS STOP

Bus Stop

Curb

The Disney Babies are spending a day at the

library. Baby Goofy is amazed at the height

of the  and the number of books. He

can't decide which one to choose. Baby Mickey

is using the  to see if the library

has one of his favorite books. Baby Gyro is looking

at a  spread on the floor. Baby Donald

and Baby Pete are quarreling because they

both want to look at the same  .

Baby Minnie and Baby Daisy like the same

 but they are sharing it.

Shelves

Card Catalogue

Magazine

Picture
Book

Newspaper

AT THE POST OFFICE

Baby Minnie has come to the post office to

mail a  . She is handing it to Baby

Goofy, who is pretending to be a mailman. He has

just put down his heavy  full of letters,

magazines and postcards. Baby Donald has found

a and is stamping everything, even Baby

Daisy's hand. Baby Gyro has bought a postage

stamp to put on a big which he has

carefully wrapped and taped. Baby Pete has found

an . He wonders what is in it, but won't

open it unless it is addressed to him.

Mailbag

Letter

Stamp

Envelope

Package

AT THE SERVICE STATION

The Disney Babies take good care of their little

cars. Baby Daisy has driven hers in so that

Baby Donald can fill the tank at the  .

Now Baby Mickey has opened the hood

to look at the  and check the oil. Baby

Gyro needs some help, because his car has

a flat  . Baby Goofy has found the leak.

Now he is refilling the tire with the  .

Poor Baby Gyro was really worried. But he is feeling

better now. Baby Minnie was nice enough to bring

him a cool drink in a .

Gas Pump

Engine

Glass

Air Hose

Tire

AT THE MALL

There are so many  and so many things to

see at a mall. The Disney Babies don't know

where to start. To go upstairs they will ride

on the  . Since Baby Goofy is always

hungry, he never looks any farther than the nearest

 . Baby Daisy was looking for a new

hair ribbon, but she has been attracted by a

window full of . All the Disney Babies

like that. There are so many kinds to choose.

Baby Mickey would like a . Do

you like to go to the mall ?

AT THE DEPARTMENT STORE

There are many things for sale at a department

store. The Disney Babies can see beautiful glass

arranged neatly on shelves. A store  displays

an elegant dress. Behind that stands a round

 with many shirts in various sizes. Baby

Goofy wonders about the piece of paper hanging

on each jacket. He doesn't know it is a  .

Many sweaters, blouses and handbags are

shown in the glass  . Other goods on

sale are piled up in boxes, like the teakettles, or set

near the counter. Do you like to shop ?

KINDS OF BUILDINGS

There are many kinds of buildings in the

city. There are fire engines in the fire

station. At the , people live with their

families. They can buy clothing and furniture

at a 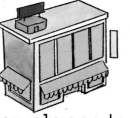 . When travelers arrive

from other places to visit a new city or town,

they stay at a  . The police, who

watch the traffic and stop crime, operate

out of a 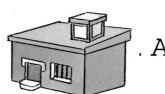 . And the government

of most cities and towns is run from the

 , where the mayor has his or her office.

City Hall

Police Station

Apartment House

Hotel

Department Store

PLACES WE GO

The Disney Babies like to think about all the

exciting places there are in the city. Baby

Donald and Baby Gyro like the big  .

Baby Daisy is remembering the afternoons she went

to the . Baby Mickey and Baby Minnie

like to go and see the paintings, costumes, Indians

and dinosaurs at the  . Baby Goofy is

excited about all the flavors of ice cream he can

get at the  . And all the Disney

Babies look forward to the day when they

will go to for the first time.

Swimming Pool

Movies

School

Museum

Ice-cream Stand

KINDS OF TRUCKS

So many kinds of trucks ! Baby Gyro is

putting trash into the  .

Baby Gus is waiting nearby with the hose

from the  . Baby Daisy's little car

has broken down, but Baby Donald will take

it to the garage with his  .

Baby Horace has unscrewed a valve to

see how much is in his .

Baby Goofy is riding in the back of his

 . What kind of truck do you like

the most ?